EDGE BOOKS

THE KIDS' GUIDE TO

DUCT TAPE

PROJECTS

by Sheri Bell-Rehwoldt

CAPSTONE PRESS

a capstone imprint

Edge Books are published by Capstone Press,
151 Good Counsel Drive, P.O. Box 669, Mankato, Minnesota 56002.
www.capstonepub.com

Library of Congress Cataloging-in-Publication Data
Bell-Rehwoldt, Sheri.
    The kids' guide to duct tape projects / by Sheri Bell-Rehwoldt.
    p. cm. — (Edge. Kids' guides)
    Includes bibliographical references and index.
    Summary: "Describes how to make duct tape projects in a step-by-step
format"—Provided by publisher.
    ISBN 978-1-4296-6010-5 (library binding)
    1. Handicraft—Juvenile literature. 2. Duct tape—Juvenile literature. I. Title.
TT160.B4556 2012
745.5—dc22   2011002485

Editorial Credits
Mandy Robbins, editor; Kyle Grenz, designer; Wanda Winch, media researcher,
    Eric Manske, production specialist; Marcy Morin, project production

Photo Credits
All photos Capstone Studio/Karon Dubke except:
Duck Tape® brand duct tape, Stuck at Prom Contest®, 23 (top); NARA/
PhoM2c. Paul Queenan, Coast Guard, 4

Printed in the United States of America in Stevens Point, Wisconsin.
032011   006111WZF11

Table of Contents

You may have heard that you can fix anything with duct tape. But did you know that you can also make fun craft projects with it?

Duct tape was invented during World War II (1939–1945). The U.S. military needed a strong, waterproof material for mending gear and equipment. Soldiers needed to be able to tear this material by hand.

Soldiers needed a tough tape that would stick well in difficult conditions.

4

The Johnson and Johnson company created a tough tape for the military. Three layers made the tape extra strong. The first layer was rubbery glue. The second was fabric **mesh**, and the top layer was plastic. The first duct tape was olive green to match military uniforms.

After World War II, home builders used the military tape to connect furnace and air conditioning pipes called ducts. People soon started calling the tape "duct tape." To match the silver ducts, the tape color was changed to shiny gray.

Today duct tape is a popular craft material. It is available in many colors. Duct tape also comes in different strengths. Strength is determined by the number of threads in the mesh layer. The more threads per inch, the stronger the tape.

« **mesh**—a net made of threads woven together with open spaces between them

Safety First

Creating duct tape crafts should be fun, not painful. Before you grab the duct tape, there are a couple safety tips you should learn.

1 You may need to cut through thick layers of duct tape. If using a scissors doesn't work, ask an adult to help you use a utility knife.

2 Never apply the tape to your body. It could rip out your hair when you peel it off. Apply duct tape over clothing, a towel, a trash bag, or a hat.

Duct Tape Fabric

Many duct tape projects require that you begin by making duct tape "fabric." To do so, you simply layer two strips of duct tape by attaching their sticky sides together. Lay strips of duct tape on a large, flat surface, sticky side up. Overlap them by 0.25 inch. Cover the sticky side with more strips, sticky side down, again overlapping by 0.25 inch. Then trim the fabric to the size you need for your project.

Metric Conversions	
0.25 in	0.6 cm

TAPING TIP: YOU COULD ALSO OVERLAP STRIPS OF DUCT TAPE ONTO A PIECE OF CLOTH. THIS GIVES YOUR DUCT TAPE FABRIC MORE FLEXIBILITY.

Book Cover

Book covers don't have to be drab brown. Duct tape book covers offer protection and give your books a look that is uniquely yours.

1 Cut down the long side of the bag. You will also need to cut off the flat bottom of the bag.

2 Lay the bag flat on the table. Place your book in the middle of the bag.

3 Fold the top and bottom edges of the paper bag. They should be slightly longer than the top and bottom edges of your book.

8

4 Fold the left edge of the bag around the front cover of the book. Then slip the book into the flap created by the top and bottom folds. Repeat for the back cover of the book.

5 Use a piece of duct tape 2 inches longer than the height of your book. Lay the strip along the cover's right edge. Leave 1 inch hanging off in all directions. Fold the edges into the inside of the book cover.

6 Slip the book out of the book cover so you don't accidentally tape the book. Continue adding duct tape strips. Overlap the strips by 0.25 inch.

7 When you've nearly covered the back, slip the book back inside the cover. Finish covering the back edge with the book inside the cover.

Metric Conversions	
0.25 in	0.6 cm
1 in	2.5 cm
2 in	5 cm

TAPING TIP: YOU CAN USE DIFFERENT COLORED TAPE TO CREATE A PATTERN OR DECORATE THE BOOK.

CELL PHONE POUCH

What You Need

* duct tape of one or more colors
* ruler
* cell phone

This nifty pouch will keep your cell phone from getting scratched. Use bright colors so you can easily find your phone.

1 Use the ruler to measure the length, width, and thickness of your phone.

2 Now create your duct tape fabric. It should be twice as long as your phone plus 1 inch. The width should be the same width as your phone, plus 1 inch.

3 Fold your fabric in half with the short edges touching. Unfold it, and draw a straight line along the crease.

4 Cut along the line 0.5 inch from each side.

5 Fold the fabric in half again. Starting at the end of each cut, make a 45-degree cut angling out.

6 Lay your phone on one half of the fabric. Fold the other half up over the phone.

7 Overlap the side edges and tape them together. Tuck the tape in at the top of your case to make a smooth edge.

8 Take your phone out of the pouch and cut a small hole at the bottom. It should be big enough so you can poke your finger in the hole to pop your phone out.

Metric Conversions	
0.5 in	1.3 cm
1 in	2.5 cm

WALLET

What You Need

* ★ one or more colors of duct tape
* ★ ruler
* ★ dollar bill
* ★ scissors

Do you have cash burning a hole in your pocket? Keep your money safe with this handy duct tape wallet.

1 Make a sheet of duct tape fabric 8 inches long and four strips wide.

2 Fold the fabric in half the long way. Tape the short sides together.

3 Make another sheet of duct tape fabric 7.5 inches long and 4 inches wide.

4 Out of the fabric, cut four rectangles. They should be 3.75 inches long and 2 inches tall. These will be pockets for any cards you may have.

5 Fold a piece of duct tape over one of the long edges of each pocket. This will give your pockets clean top edges. Trim any excess tape.

6 About 0.5 inch down from the top of your wallet, line up two of the pockets. There should be one pocket on each side of your wallet. The clean edges should be on the top. Leave a 0.25 inch space between the pockets so the wallet folds properly.

Metric Conversions	
0.25 in	0.6 cm
0.5 in	1.3 cm
2 in	5 cm
3.75 in	9.5 cm
4 in	10.2 cm
7.5 in	19 cm
8 in	20.3 cm
8.5 in	21.6 cm

7 Use two overlapping strips of duct tape 8.5 inches long to tape on your pockets.

continue on next page

8 Place the second two pockets 0.5 inch below the first two pockets. Again, the clean edges should be on top.

9 Use two overlapping strips of duct tape 8.5 inches long to tape on your pockets. Trim off all extra tape so the wallet edges are neat and smooth.

Metric Conversions

0.5 in	1.3 cm
8.5 in	21.6 cm

10 Close the wallet by folding the two ends together. The pockets are now tucked inside.

11 Now you can fill up your wallet and head to the mall!

FLOWER POWER

What You Need

* scissors
* plastic drinking straw
* green duct tape
* another colored duct tape

Do you want to cheer up a friend when she's feeling down? Send her duct tape roses. Unlike the real thing, these blooms will last forever.

STEM

1 Cut a piece of green duct tape slightly longer than your straw.

2 Lay the tape flat on a table, with the sticky side up. Lay the straw along one of the long edges of the tape. Roll the straw toward the opposite edge so that the tape tightly wraps around the straw.

ROSEBUD

1 Cut a 3-inch piece of colored duct tape. Lay it down with the sticky side up. Fold the top corners in until they meet in the middle.

2 Wrap the sticky side of the tape around the end of the straw with the point facing up. This is your rosebud.

Metric Conversions

3 in	7.6 cm

continue on next page

PETALS

1 Cut a 3-inch piece of colored duct tape the same color as the rosebud. Lay it down with the sticky side up. Fold the top edge down, leaving a small amout of sticky tape.

2 Cut the folded edge in an arch shape.

3 Tape the petal around the base of the rosebud. Try to pucker the petal out as you tape it on.

4 Repeat steps 1 through 3 to make more petals. Stagger the petals as you put them on. Ten petals is usually enough to make a beautiful rose.

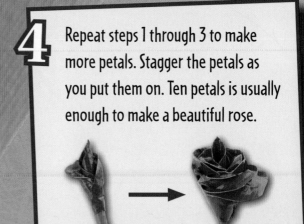

TAPING TIP: TO GIVE YOUR FLOWERS FRAGRANCE, SPRITZ THEM WITH PERFUME.

LEAVES

1 Cut a 3-inch piece of green duct tape. Lay it down sticky-side-up. Fold the top corners in until they meet in the middle. This will be a leaf.

2 You will need two or three leaves to cover the base of the flower petals. Attach the leaves to the base of the flower.

Metric Conversions	
3 in	7.6 cm

TAPING TIP: MAKE AN ENTIRE DUCT TAPE BOUQUET, AND DECORATE A VASE WITH DUCT TAPE.

FRAME IT!

What You Need
* duct tape
* greeting card
* string
* photo
* scissors

The best part of taking pictures is displaying them. You can combine old birthday cards with duct tape to create your own picture frames.

1 Make sure your card is at least 0.5 inch longer and wider than your photo.

18

3 Remove the photo and draw a second rectangle inside the first. It should be about 0.25 inch smaller. Cut along the inner line to make a hole for your photo.

2 Open the card. Lay the photo in the middle, and trace around it.

Metric Conversions	
0.25 in	.6 cm
0.5 in	1.3 cm

4 Cover the front and back of the card entirely in duct tape. Wrap the tape carefully around the inner edges of the photo hole.

5 Tape your photo inside the hole with the image facing out.

6 Slip the string through the fold of the card, and fold the card shut.

7 Tape the bottom edges and one side of the card together. Leave the other side open so you can easily change your photo whenever you want to.

8 Tie the string in a knot and hang your picture wherever you want.

TAPING TIP: YOU CAN DECORATE THE FRAME WITH GLITTER, MARKERS, OR STICKERS.

CHECKERBOARD

What You Need

* black and red duct tape
* plastic trash bag
* scissors
* thin marker
* ruler
* cardboard (optional)

Who doesn't love a game of checkers?
Now you can play on a board you made yourself!

2 Tape nine **horizontal** strips of black and red duct tape on the bag. The strips should be 16 inches long. Alternate the colors and be sure not to overlap the strips.

1 Tape the trash bag flat on your work surface.

3 Lay the ruler **vertically** across your strips and mark lines down the tape as wide as your duct tape roll.

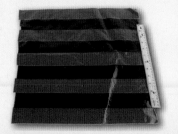

4 Cut along the lines so that you have eight separate rows.

« **horizontal**—flat and parallel to the ground
« **vertical**—straight up and down

5 Create a sticky sheet of duct tape about 20 inches long and 20 inches wide. Do this by overlapping strips of duct tape with their sticky sides up.

6 Create your checkerboard grid by laying the red and black strips over the sticky fabric. Arrange the strips so that the squares alternate red and black squares.

7 Once you have all eight strips down, trim the excess. Tape a thin strip of black tape around the edge of your board.

Metric Conversions	
16 in	41 cm
20 in	51 cm

TAPING TIP: YOU CAN MAKE CHECKER PIECES BY COVERING CARDBOARD CIRCLES WITH RED AND BLACK DUCT TAPE.

FASHION-FORWARD VEST

What You Need

* old T-shirt
* two colors of duct tape
* thin marker
* scissors
* stapler

Vests have been a fashion trend for decades. Make a fashion statement by hitting the halls in a custom-made duct tape vest.

1 Lay your shirt flat, and tape the edges down on your work surface so it doesn't move. Draw a pattern for the vest on the front of the shirt. Do your best to make sure the sides are even.

2 Cut along the lines you drew. Then cut down the shoulder and side seams. Now your T-shirt is cut into three pieces.

STUCK AT THE PROM

Teenagers in the United States can enter a yearly "Stuck at Prom" contest. The students enter the contest by making their prom outfits from duct tape! The contest was first held in 2000. High school students who enter the contest compete for a college **scholarship**. Their outfits don't have to be made entirely from duct tape, but part of the judging is based on how much duct tape is used.

23

3 Cover the outside of your vest pieces with duct tape. Neatly trim the edges.

« **scholarship**–a grant of money that helps a student pay for education costs

continue on next page

4 Lay the back vest piece flat with the duct tape side facing up. Lay your side pieces on top of the back piece with the duct tape side facing down. Trim any excess to make sure the edges match perfectly.

5 Staple the shoulder and side seams together. Place several strips of duct tape over the staples.

6 Now turn the vest right-side-out. Use strips of duct tape around any unfinished edges to give your vest a finished look. You could use a different color for this piping.

CAP IT!

What You Need

* old baseball cap
* folder
* stapler
* pencil
* duct tape
* scissors

What fashion accessory goes best with a duct tape vest? A duct tape cap!

1 Your baseball hat is made up of six **arch**-shaped triangle pieces. Cut out one of the triangles.

2 Trace the triangle on your folder. Around your traced triangle, draw another triangle about 0.25 inches bigger. Cut out the larger triangle. This is your pattern.

Metric Conversions

0.25 in	0.6 cm

3 Make six pieces of duct tape fabric in the shape of your pattern piece. You can use any colors you like.

« **arch**—a curved line or shape

continue on next page

4 Fold a piece of tape over the bottom edge of each triangle. This will give your cap a clean edge.

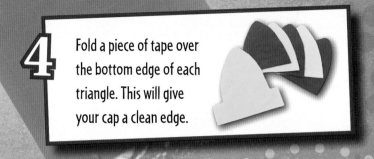

5 Lay two of your duct tape triangles back-to-back and staple one long edge together.

6 Unfold the two triangles so that the staples are in back.

7 Lay another triangle on top of one of the stapled triangles. Staple the other edge of the first triangle to the edge of the third triangle.

8 Continue stapling the edges together until all six triangles are stapled together. The staples should be on the outside of the cap.

9 Use strips of duct tape to cover the staples.

10 Turn your hat inside out.

11 Cut off the bill of your model hat and trace it onto a folder. Cut out this shape.

continue on next page

27

12 Cover the cardboard in strips of duct tape and trim the edges.

13 Attach four strips of duct tape, about 2 inches long, to the underside of the bill. Line up the bill with the front of the hat and press the tape firmly to the inside of the hat.

14 Trace a quarter onto the duct tape roll. Cut the circle out, and tape it to the top of the hat for a finishing touch.

TAPING TIP: TO ADJUST THE SIZE OF THE HAT, CUT A GAP IN THE BACK. TAPE A THIN STRIP OF DUCT TAPE FABRIC TO ONE SIDE OF THE GAP. TAPE THE OTHER SIDE OF THE STRIP TO THE OTHER SIDE OF THE GAP. ADJUST THE STRIP TO FIT YOUR HEAD.

Metric Conversions	
2 in	5 cm

KEEP TAPING!

Now that you've learned some basic duct tape projects, keep taping. You can even come up with your own creations. Your imagination is the only limit when it comes to duct tape!

GLOSSARY

arch (ARCH)—a curved line or shape

horizontal (hor-uh-ZON-tuhl)—flat and parallel to the ground

mesh (MESH)—a net made of threads woven together with open spaces between them

scholarship (SKOL-ur-ship)—a grant of money that helps a student pay for education costs

vertical (VUR-tuh-kuhl)—straight up and down

Sarkady, Nick. *Trash to Toys.* Springville, Utah: Bonneville Books, 2010.

Trusty, Brad, and Cindy Trusty. *The Kids' Guide to Balloon Twisting.* Kids' Guides. Mankato, Minn.: Capstone Press, 2011.

INTERNET SITES

FactHound offers a safe, fun way to find Internet sites related to this book. All of the sites on FactHound have been researched by our staff.

Here's all you do:

Visit *www.facthound.com*

Type in this code: 9781429660105

Super-cool stuff!

Check out projects, games and lots more at
www.capstonekids.com

INDEX

32